Altars

Mary Elizabeth Smith

Cover Painting: *Silent Madonna* by Elizabeth Chapin
Painting Photographer: Patty Clark

For Christine and John

A quiet place to find your truth

Mary Elizabeth Smith

*Thanks for "Lifting the Veil" so we could
see paridise – Think it
will be like this in heaven!
We fell in love with
you both*

In appreciation to those who faithfully traveled this road with me, I give thanks for:

Jane Gerber, my flower partner and friend since we were 28 years old, who assisted me in writing and editing page after page.

Jane Hope, my sister, who suggested I include cherished quotes that I have collected through the years.

Elizabeth Chapin, my daughter, who allowed her painting for the front cover, and rearranged, for the better, many words and thoughts.

Joe Rankin, a friend and flower partner these last 6 years, whose giftedness, vision, talent, and creativity stretches and challenges me.

George, my husband and companion for fifty years, who blesses me constantly and affirms my creative gifts.

ISBN 978-1-938819-00-1

www.altarsbook.com

Sixth Edition - November 2013

PRINTED BY ALPHAGRAPHICS OF PEARL, MS

When I was young, I knew intuitively that the church altar was the visible part of worship, as it is the first thing people see when they arrive, providing a powerful "aha" moment even before the music begins, taking their hearts to God as the prelude to worship. For the past 35 years, one of my greatest joys has been to think about, plan, and place flowers on church altars Sunday after Sunday with gifted artists along side of me.

Most churches in the United States are not blessed by the amazing gothic architecture of Europe where just entering the sanctuary focuses one's soul and mind on God. However, I realized early that our greatest artist, our CREATOR, gives us many textures, interesting wild flowers along the highways, like Queen Anne's lace and lime green dock, growing together. Being drawn to God's creations in nature helped me to see things with a fresh eye and to bring wild plants and weeds into altar arrangements in unexpected ways. I decided the scale and simplicity of flowers could help substitute for what was missing in some of our more modern sanctuaries.

Because one cannot improve on nature's design, it became a goal of mine that a first glance at the altar would give the viewer a feeling of the goodness and grace of God, not who did the arrangement.

This collection of my favorite designs has been amassed over many years. I am sharing it now hoping to give new and inspiring ideas on available yard flowers and, perhaps, a new and different sense of scale. My sister encouraged me to incorporate quotes, so the book could be a blessing to people unable to get to their church of choice, as well as altar guilds and church flower committees. The quotes, some of my favorites collected through the years, have meant as much to me as the photographs.

Psalms 46:10
Be still and know that I am God
Be still and know that I am
Be still and know
Be still
Be

In our busy, noisy world that is all about DOING, we rush around frantically and at the end of the day are still spinning and wondering why we are empty, dissatisfied, and unfulfilled, like there is a "hole in our souls". Recently I heard Susanne Stabile say, "We need to come to the knowledge and truth that MY LIFE IS NOT ABOUT ME!" We have an opportunity to be still each day and be with God, so our lives will reflect something bigger and grander than ourselves, reflecting HIS LIGHT for a broken and hurting world. There is more than learning ABOUT God, there is that Holy moment when we can actually be with Him. May this not just be a book to be looked at once, but a tool to help be STILL, and KNOW, and BE each day.

I hope this book will help you to reflect upon, remember, and feel the loving presence of our good and generous God.

Mary Elizabeth Smith

The book is ordered by the beautiful disciplines of the liturgical Christian calendar.
Year after year, never changing, we retrace the path of redemption:

Advent – the season of waiting
Christmastide – celebrate Jesus' birth
Epiphany – when we remember that Jesus came to, and for, the whole wide World
Lent – the somber season including Palm Sunday and Holy Week
Eastertide – hope filled joy
Pentecost – soul stirring season
Time after Pentecost
Ordinary time
Christ the King Sunday - final Sunday of the church calendar
Another Advent – opening another year, year upon year, generation upon Generation

Charles Poole 2009

Liturgical Year

Advent: A season of waiting for Christ to come.

The long slow purple and rose comma at which we pause before the red and green exclamation point of Christmas.

A season to ponder the first coming of our Lord.

The moment when as Frederick Buechner says, "The whole world holds its breath."

The Sunday before we set our feet to a quiet path of waiting that will take us back to the first coming and forward to the next.

Charles Poole

Angels fly because they
take themselves lightly.

G.K. Chesterton

Churches should be
Arm in Arm if not
Eye to Eye.

David Redding

John 3:16

God - the greatest lover

So loved - the greatest degree

The world - the greatest company

That He gave - the greatest act

His only begotten Son - the greatest gift

That whosoever - the greatest opportunity

Believeth - the greatest simplicity

In Him - the greatest attraction

Should not perish - the greatest promise

But - the greatest difference

Have - the greatest certainty

Eternal life - the greatest possession

Davies

Move about this world more slowly and carefully, and silence in us any voice other than yours!

Jill Barnes Buckley

We are not here to see through each other;
we are here to see each other through.

Charles Poole

The truth will set you free....
But first it will make you mad.

Ernest Campbell

Pain takes you places joy
tried to but never could.

Charles Poole

Listen with Holy Spirit-filled ears.
From: Laity Lodge

13

No one remembers what you say; they remember how you made them feel.

Author Unknown

I'm not called to be successful; I am called to be faithful.

Mother Teresa

Prayer is standing in the presence of God with the mind in the heart.

Desert Fathers and Mothers

Prayer: "A child-like quiet in the Lap of God."

Mark Roberts, Laity Lodge

God doesn't answer everything we ask for, but He gives us a lot more than we know.

Charles Poole

I discover who I am through the mirror of your eyes.

Eddie Spencer

How you are acting is speaking so loudly I can not hear what you are saying.

An AA Quote

Vocation: The place God calls you is the place where your deep gladness and the world's deep hunger meet.

Frederick Buechner

To not follow the call is to **under live** the only life you will ever have.

Charles Poole

19

Psalm 100

On your feet now - applaud God! Bring a gift of laughter, sing yourselves into His presence. Enter with the password; "Thank You!" Make yourselves at home, talking praise, thank Him, worship Him.

Eugene Peterson, The Message

"Leave your children vision. Leave them able to do something with their hands and their own hearts."

Author Unknown

Choose your hill to die on!
Earl Palmer
Don't let others steal your joy!
Guy Parker
Gently detach from toxic people.
Guy Parker

INTEGRITY is when your insides match your outsides.

Judy Parker

INTEGRITY can be neither lost nor concealed nor faked nor quenched nor outlived, nor, I believe, in the long run, denied.

Eudora Welty

Good Friday

When you mimic the original designer, God, and bring nature to the altar in a simple way, that can be a most powerful visual experience in worship.

Faith never knows where it is being led, but it knows and loves the One who is leading.

Oswald Chambers

Humans are the only thing God did not finish...
He allows us to finish our own creation .

Frank Pollard

When you remember me, it means that you have carried something of who I am with you, that I have left some mark of who I am on who you are... For as long as you remember me, I am never entirely lost. If you forget me, part of who I am will be gone.

Frederick Buechner

God will give us the strength to walk and not faint. But if we do faint, if we do stagger, collapse, stumble and fall, God will curl up next to us until we can get up and start out all over again.

Charles Poole

Happiness now is worth the pain later.
C.S. Lewis' wife, Joy

Pain now is worth the happiness then.
C.S. Lewis after his wife's death
"Shadowlands"

The only true love is people who love people to God.
Kierkegaard

Jesus calls us to the reality that life can only be lived forward. NO REWIND BUTTON!

Richard Rohr

Forgetting the past, I press forward.

PHILIPPIANS (Paul)

The one prayer God will never answer is prayer for an encore.....God simply will not give us the good old days - Rather, God will give us food for new days.

C.S. Lewis

A good marriage is more than finding the right person, it is being the right person!

We have a God-shaped opening in us.

Pascal

There is a difference in doing church work...and the work of the church.
Our church is not liberal or conservative...but transforming.

Roger Paynter

I'm walking in my garden, and all of a sudden over night, something has bloomed - maybe the honeysuckle, maybe the roses, or maybe it's just the cabbage in the vegetable garden. And I don't ever see it, but know it's present. I feel its presence. No, I smell its presence. I'm aware of it. For many of us that's an experience like that of experiencing God in prayer.

from Vigen Guroian

Mother's Day

Worship does not mean offering flowers. It means offering your heart to the vast mystery of the universe. It means letting your heart pulse with the life of the universe, without thought and without reservation. It means being so in love that you are willing to dissolve and be recreated in every moment.

Author Unknown

44

I think God wanted his people to build altars for THEIR sake, something that would help them remember something they could look back on and remember the time they were rescued, or they were given grace.

Donald Miller

May the Lord bless you and keep
you.
May the Lord's face shine upon you
and be gracious to you.
May God give you grace not to sell
yourself short:
Grace to risk something big for
something good:
Grace to remember that the world is
now too dangerous for anything but
truth, and too small for anything but
love.
So may God take your minds and
think through them.
May God take your lips and speak
through them.
May God take your hands
and work through them.
May God take your hearts and set
them on fire.

Roger Paynter

There are two kinds of people; People with problems and.....Liars!

When God hates all the same people that you do - you can be
confident that you have created God in your Image!

Anne Lamott

We live our lives in chapters. If you are stuck in this chapter, start the next one.

Elta Trueblood (Quaker)

Running away from home is not all that uncommon. Sometimes we run away from home without leaving. We just conveniently aren't there for others.

Macrina Wiederkehr

Practice the presence of Christ.
Ponder the Scriptures.
Pray daily in private.
Serve others in Jesus' name, and

Withhold no good deed, spiritual or financial,
from widows and orphans,
the poor and oppressed.

As you live this way,
you will find those most needy of God,
you will find yourself
and you will be found.

Stan Wilson

You may not get your miracles, but there's always a ram in the bush.

Hellen Taliaferro

Evolution is how it happened. Creation is why.
Earl Palmer

Even should we find another Eden, we would not be fit to enjoy it perfectly nor stay in it forever.

Henry van Dyke

A saint: a life-giver.

Frederick Buechner

A Saint: one who exaggerates what the world neglects.

G.K. Chesterton

Father's Day

The Great Commandment is not 'Thou shalt be *right*.'
The Great Commandment is to 'be in love.'

Author Unknown

Happiness depends on Holiness.
William Faulkner

Laughter is carbonated Holiness!
Anne Lamott

God sometimes does less than we hoped, but God always does more than we know.

Charles Poole

Sisters and Brothers:
We are **not** dismissed.
We are **not** just free to go.
Christ sends us!
Go to help and heal in all you do.
And may the blessing of God,
Creator, Redeemer, and Sustainer
Be with you and remain with you always.
Amen.

Jill Barnes Buckley

The Church..."a community capable of absorbing our grief."
Stanley Hauerwas

It is true that relationships are a whole lot messier than rules, but rules will never give you answers to the deep questions of the heart and they will never love you.

William Young, <u>The Shack</u>

Trinity Sunday

My work is my interruptions.
Henri Nouwen
Sometimes our best work is..."A task within a task."
Laity Lodge

70

Watch for daily visitations from God.　　　　Don't talk unless it improves the silence.

Macrina Wiederkehr

May you have the eyes to see that no visitor arrives
without a gift and no guest leaves without a blessing.
John O'Donohue, <u>To Bless the Space Between Us</u>

Don't let the logistics of your lives eclipse relationships.
Elizabeth Chapin

Grace enters the soul by a wound.
Paula D'Arcy

If your body is no longer serving you well, step out of it and go on with life.
Barbara Brown Taylor

Christ the King
Sunday

Last step of the year we:
Recall, Revisit, Rehearse, Remember
First step of the year we:
Wonder, Anticipate, Imagine, Dream, Hope.

Charles Poole

Now go from this table
To all your other tables;
Resting yourselves in the love of God,
Casting your cares upon the grace of God,
Placing your lives in the hands of God,
The hands that will hold you,
And never let you go.

Charles Poole

INFORMATION ABOUT THE PHOTOS IN THE BOOK
(Except where otherwise noted, all photos are taken at Northminster Baptist Church in Jackson, Mississippi)

Front of the book: "THE SILENT MADONNA" was painted by my talented daughter, Elizabeth Chapin, while she was an undergraduate at UVA. I feel it is a good reminder for silence in this oh-so-noisy world.

Page 1) Advent wreath: It was a tradition in Northminster Baptist Church before I joined twenty years ago. I had never seen one so full and important looking. I love the contrasting textures of the shiny magnolia leaves that are native to Mississippi mixed with the airy pine. The fat heavy candles look wonderful with it. The wreath seems to announce the importance of its message. Constructed by Northminster Flower Committee.

Page 2) My creative friend Joe Rankin, who is a member of my Sunday School class and who loves many of the same things I do, created this arrangement. It is so powerful, with the large onyx stone rising up like the root of Jesse. It says something important to all eyes – not necessarily the same to each person, but unforgettable to all.

Page 3) European Cathedral in Prague: I remember looking at this cathedral and realizing it had no need of decoration; the architecture says it all. Everyone feels that this is a sacred holy space. One candle is enough.

Page 4) St. James Episcopal Church, Jackson, MS: I did these flowers for a wedding. The lace altar cloth, which I found years ago in France, has the initials JHS, which stands for "in His steps" in Greek. Queen Anne's lace, bells of Ireland, white hydrangeas, and white larkspur are the flowers.

Page 5) Briarwood Presbyterian Church: These were done one Easter Sunday by Briarwood Church flower committee members. I chose this photo because of the rhythm and freedom expressed in the way they placed the lilies, hydrangeas, roses, white snapdragons, and greenery with interesting textures. The arching branches are Lady Banks rose greenery. To me it expresses joy.

Pages 6-7) This star burst of bittersweet and safflower says hallelujah to me – a grand Christmas statement announcing a surprise about to happen.

Page 8) A cathedral in Berlin: The very high Gothic ceiling moves one's heart upward. The very small bowl of flowers says, "Something a alive and well here".

Page 9) I did this simple altar, first covering it with an antique lace runner. The stone Madonna was created by Mildred Wolfe, a famous Jackson artist. The open Bible is flanked by two very simple glass vases mirroring three white Dutch iris, stately and strong with the surprise of grasses bending over to give it grace.

Page 10-11) During Lent we use all purple flowers and candles until Palm Sunday. The substantial gray stone pot holds the lilac branches that meander over the altar, telling a story bigger than life. The drama is a foreshadowing of what is to come. Arranged by Anne Vickery of Northminster flower committee.

Page 12) During Holy Week Joe Rankin set this bust of Christ with real planted pansies in a flat rock container. His sad face sets the tone of the week.

Page 13) Another unusual treatment by Joe Rankin, this time using his white bark container with purple wisteria draping sadly along with moss, looking like tears. Then springing forth at the top, dogwood denotes new life. For me, this magnificent arrangement makes the mind contemplate the meaning of Lent.

Page 14) Joe Rankin used this piece of driftwood as a container for potted blue hyacinth with gray moss covering the dirt. The surprise touch of green so welcome in early is a button fern.

Page 15) Potted asters are used here, but the thing which lifts it above the ordinary is the use of a green plant with round leaves in the foreground.

Page 16-17) Palm Sunday I paired my antique pottery crock with a gold ball and cross by an artist from New Orleans. My graphic artist faded the edges of this photograph, echoing the faded edges of the cover photo.

Page 18-19) Palm Sunday displays from other years done by various members of the committee. I did the one on the far right – a simple glass vase with only one palmetto palm.

Page 20) Another Palm Sunday composition, including a statue which looks like a celebration of Jesus' triumphal entry into Jerusalem – probably His happiest day, and maybe the only day He felt appreciated and as if His followers "got it". I wanted the children of the church to feel it was an exciting time, and never to forget this statue of the joyous lady loving a parade!

Page 21) On Palm Sunday the children of First Baptist Church, Austin, Texas, like those of many churches, parade down the aisle waving palm branches in an exciting and joyful celebration. I feel that my grandchildren, pictured here, will probably remember it all their lives, as will other children who are able to participate in churches across our nation.

Page 22-23) Joe Rankin filled these vases, which sit at different angles, with calla lilies, palms, and one broad flat leaf. I loved the one that had spilled out or fallen over. I passed this picture around my Sunday School class asking for comments on the symbolism. Among the wonderful theological insights, my favorite was: In life we all have weak times where we stumble and fall, but people are there with you in the church to help you up and give you another chance.

Page 24) My yard helper, named Toe, helped me put this arrangement together. He cut bamboo in our yard and helped me tie the pieces with hemp rope to make three crosses symbolic of Golgotha. I put wheat grass I had grown in containers at the base of each cross. Ordinarily good photography is never backlit, but the powerful effect created by backlighting these crosses made me include it in the book.

Page 25) I did this for outside foyer with the same jugs and dogwood that was polite enough to bloom on Easter Sunday.

Page 26) Lisa Kelly combined snowball viburnum and English dogwood. The contrast of giant and small flowers in all white seems to sing "Christ the Lord is Risen Today... Alleluia!"

Page 27) Large velvety artichoke leaves from my yard anchor this arrangement of airy Queen Anne's lace and Dutch iris with striped green and white grass, all of it punctuated by the bold Louisiana iris foliage in back. The heavy candlesticks and my heavy bowl sit on the delicate lace cloth, a nice surprise.

Page 28) Normally I do not like "overdone" flowers, but this is one of the favorite Easter arrangements I have ever done. The three vases bursting with abundance shout the good news that Easter is the most important day ever! The matched vases on the ends of the table are filled with button spirea, white larkspur, asparagus fern, and one lily each. What makes it work for me is that I only used one kind of flower – dogwood – in the center vase. The altar cloth, a piece of art itself, is handmade French lace depicting the life of Christ during Holy Week. As in many of the photographs, table cloths, vases, and other objects from home enhance the meaning of the work.

Page 29) A close-up of the dogwood in the center vase, looking just like it grows on the tree.

Page 30) Our flower committee takes donations for Easter lilies given in memory or in honor of people. In the picture on the left, the potted lilies and a rough wooden cross line the baptistry. The picture on the right shows potted lilies with rye grass displayed on a round stand in the foyer.

Page 31) This is a close up of the one pictured on page 28, pointing out the drama of not too many flowers. Simple is better.

Page 32) On Easter Sunday the families of the church bring flowers to decorate the large wooden cross which is out front for anyone passing by to see. We have an Easter breakfast and no Sunday School that day, so families can gather between the services to decorate the cross. A chicken wire cover on the cross enables even the youngest children to be successful in helping place flowers. In the picture to the right, India Smith, my youngest granddaughter, happily cradles her baby doll in one arm while getting ready to put a daffodil on the cross.

Page 33) Covenant Presbyterian Church, Jackson, MS. My friends Linda Lambeth and Susan Brown, who had just taken a class in flower arranging, created this masterpiece with a circle of vines covering vines. White hydrangeas, Queen Anne's lace, and white larkspur burst forth from the base of the circle. The "works" are covered by green moss and aspidistra leaves. This one would be excellent for a wedding.

Page 34) Joe Rankin used the stark contrast of a hard heavy container with the natural airy openness of dogwood.

Page 35) Left: European church with modest bunch of gladiolus that just add a spark to a much grander centerpiece. Top right: English dogwood fills vase photographed from behind the altar. Lower right: white apple blossoms bring the glad tidings of spring!

Page 36) Lida Carraway, one of our youngest flower committee members, filled this clear vase with hydrangeas of three colors and then added the water. The off-center placement of the evergreen wisteria gives rhythm and design. One of my favorite parts of this journey is mentoring young people like Lida, giving them the encouragement and confidence that they, too, can make "Holy Happenings".

Page 37) Limelight hydrangeas from my yard combine with loquat in this pair of vases with open Bible in the center. Light hitting clear vases and edges of hydrangeas adds drama.

Page 38) Joe Rankin used artifacts from home to set the stage for this Mother's Day arrangement. An antique runner, stone Madonna, and contemporary rock container – hard bold surfaces – contrast with lace inset cloth and frothy Queen Anne's lace and moss. We typically use white flowers on the altar for Mother's Day.

Page 39) On a table in the foyer the same Mother's Day, my statue accompanies a cross I made with three shades of hydrangea blossoms, one scabiosa bud, and the magically light touch of maidenhair fern. The disc on which the arrangement rests is an old rusty plow disc, partially gilded and turned into an unconventional container by Dean and Jane Gerber.

Page 40-41) This composition of six vases of the same color, but different shapes and heights, I arranged with different colors and flowers at the entrance to a sanctuary to welcome people arriving for a wedding.

Page 42) An unusual container, but perfect for its height and white color on a spring day, this umbrella stand is filled with lavender and white Queen Anne's lace, repeating the color of the container.

Page 43) Joe Rankin inverted a vase and attached a glass bowl to the top to hold the water for his draping potted plant. He used water picks to add the red bud branches from the woods. Another creative touch was the use of important looking vases as candle holders.

Page 44) Here electric lime-green buds of snowball viburnum are accented by fancy-leaf elephant ears and variegated grass, all from my yard. The umbrella stand does service as a vase atop a Plexiglas piece that protects the two cloths draped over the table side by side.

Page 45) Briarwood Presbyterian Church: As a memorial for my long-time mentor, I arranged limelight hydrangeas, purple agapanthus, variegated grass, and the gracefully draping bear grass in a rustic white urn. The filet crochet altar cloth bears the Christian symbols of cross and dove.

Page 46) Here I established the main line with a banana tree branch from my yard and added rattlesnake ginger and rostrata hanging heliconia which cascades down its stem, giving a happy effect. Other greenery from my yard adds weight at the bottom.

Page 47) Joe Rankin made a simple statement using only one branch from a banana tree with his wonderful green pottery containers. He turned two pottery vases upside down, attached pillar candles, and covered the joint with gray moss.

Page 48) Left: In high summer using my white vases with shades of green had a cooling effect. Cracked geodes on the table add weight and interest. Fancy elephant ears, Louisiana iris leaves, and variegated grasses, cleome blossoms, and a few limelight hydrangea blossoms give a mixture of textures and shapes. Top right: A single magnolia blossom, cut that morning since they turn brown easily. Lower right: Small yard hydrangeas are used with cascading green sea oats.

Page 49) Another European altar with ornate carvings, arches and reliefs surrounding it and small arrangement not attempting to compete with the magnificent background.

Page 50) Oak leaf hydrangeas from my yard, trying hard to imitate the way they grow on the bush, fill these favorite urns.

Page 51) This stunning asymmetrical display by Joe Rankin includes split leaf philodendron, their glossy leaves catching the light, palm fronds, French tulips, white lilies, and snow white hydrangeas. The candlesticks are marble pillars.

Page 52) Left: My favorite blown glass container is so high drama it needs only a simple branch of magnolia with one open flower and two buds. Upper right: Joe Rankin filled his cross vase with green goddess callas and green hypericum berries. Lower right: Joe surrounded an artichoke with green spider mums and fatsia leaves.

Page 53) Left: Joe Rankin created a perfect example of using nothing but greenery for a dramatic effect. Variegated hosta leaves, aspidistra leaves, and three papyrus grass poms catch the light. Right: Magnolia leaves that have been shined spill out of a stone urn. Only the pod at the base shows the red seeds for one touch of color.

Page 54) Left: Cattails seem masculine to me, so I particularly like to use them on Father's Day. Here I thrust them into my antique jug. Right: Lovely eggplants of various colors are piled on a plate. Behind them, one stalk of cattail is placed off center in a white vase to add height.

Page 55) This tailored treatment of the altar for Father's Day seems to reflect men's strength and dependability. In the center, "The Fathers Word".

Page 56-57) My tubular steel vases, painted white here, echo the pipes of our organ. They fill the altar along with some white vases. Flowers used are vibrant zinnias, variegated grass (which picks up the white in the vases), and assorted leaves and ferns.

Page 58) Briarwood Presbyterian Church, Jackson, MS: Arranged by their flower committee, this is a memorial tribute to a longtime member who loved to farm and hunt. Wheat and sunflowers, which he grew on his farm, fill a rough wooden basket. A few pheasant feathers, an allusion to his love of hunting, spike up from the basket. A hand-woven raw silk runner in fall colors spills out and around the basket, along with gourds grown on his farm by his grandson.

Page 59) The sunflowers in this majestic celebration of fall were furnished by my husband George from his hunting camp. I think it makes a statement that God is full of surprises.

Page 60) Only a simple bunch of roses on an ornate European altar reminds the visitor that someone lovingly placed the flowers recently.

Page 61) Left: This asymmetrical delight created by Joe Rankin mixes just-turning gingko leaves with rust colored cypress, picking up the tone of the vase. Gourds on the table repeat the colors. Right: A magnificent green glass jar is filled with fall foliage and placed on a needlepoint runner.

Page 62) I was commissioned to do this arrangement as a memorial for one of the founders of our church. Pointing up to heaven, it is a celebration of a huge life well lived. The candlesticks on the sides are wooden ones which I finished with gold leaf.

Page 63) Dietrich Bonhoffer's church in Germany, refreshing and stunning in its simplicity.

Page 64) This mixture of ornamental grasses is an excellent way to announce the beginning of autumn.

Page 65) Using the same setting as on the preceding page, I filled the vase with pampas grass along with some bear grass for grace. I have learned to spray the plumes of grasses or cattails with heavy hair spray or matte polyurethane to prevent shedding. This is also a good treatment for goldenrod.

Page 66) This was one of my first Thanksgiving altar arrangements. I used an old torn stair runner on the table and arranged fall leaves and glossy gourds on it. The darker leaves are low in the arrangement and the lighter gingko leaves rise above them, making the statement only they can make. I painted the dragonfly on the shiny red gourd. The caramel colored candles and dark wood candlesticks seem so right for fall. The bud vase with a white rosebud on the left end of the table is there to announce the birth of a new baby in our congregation.

Page 67) Briarwood Presbyterian Church, Jackson, MS: Jane Gerber arranged this explosion of fall colored leaves, lilies, and mums in her copper wash pot. The fall vegetables and fruits on the table add texture and shape to delight the eye.

Page 68) For Trinity Sunday I selected three identical urns and placed in each a stalk of variegated cane from my yard. I used some banana leaves, fatsia, and split-leaf philodendron at the bases to keep them from looking top-heavy.

Page 69) Using three ordinary buckets from home on a matching oval tray, I filled each bucket with a separate arrangement, but they all work together as a whole. I love the single stately iris. I wanted this to be a statement of vertical lines with mushrooms and kumquats at the base. I used a few fatsia leaves down low and lots of tall thin equisetum, also known as mule tail or horse tail.

Page 70) Let the light come in on this simple display of autumn leaves and berries, flanked by two antique Beidemeyer candlesticks, giving a "different twist" to the table.

Page 71) I started with a table cloth I made from four yards of fabric and then completely covered the altar with leaves and gourds. Note the high gloss on the gourds in contrast to the leaves. The two burnt orange candles repeat the colors of the leaves and also add gloss. Pheasant feathers provide a third vertical shaft in an otherwise horizontal presentation.

Page 72) Left: Because I always cut my grasses just before the first freeze, I gathered most of one clump into this low bowl with moss around the base. The antique cloth with inserted tatted cross is one I bought on a trip to the Holy Land. Right: My lace cloth and favorite silver basket from home provide the right setting for these oak leaf hydrangeas.

Page 73) Left: This three-foot long Plexiglas container is just wide and deep enough for a row of wet Oasis. This one is framed by gilded wooden molding, but the clear container can be used without the frame, adding Galax leaves or moss to cover the works. The flowers, of varying heights, seem to sprout up as if in a garden. Here I used larkspur, iris, and hydrangea. Right: Jane Gerber did this lily arrangement for a wedding at Briarwood Presbyterian Church. Arching branches of eleagnus give it grace and rhythm, while spears of white larkspur give a touch of whimsy. The wedding banner can be seen in the background.

Page 74) Chapel of the Cross, Madison, MS: Irene Crowder created all three of these arrangements at this very old church. Upper left: The altar is covered with masses of white and yellow lilies. Lower left: The same flowers rise in tree form in a corner of the sanctuary. Right: This is a nice juxtaposition of a modern-looking arrangement of lilies and greenery in front of the old wavy glass window.

Page 75) Filling the matching vases with budding nandina gives a simple background to the white lilies.

Page 76) St. Andrews Episcopal Church, Jackson, MS: This magnificent carved, waxed, walnut background asks that the flowers be traditional. Left: Done by the head of the St. Andrews altar guild. Right: Jane Gerber and I did for a funeral there, being careful to obey their rule that no flower should extend higher than the arms of the cross.

Page 77) Christ the King Sunday, the last Sunday of the liturgical year, is always the Sunday before advent begins. This altar is at First Presbyterian in Nashville, TN. The scale of this is as important as the Sunday and the height of the arrangement is perfect.

Page 78) This is a concrete nativity scene on a table in my courtyard at home showing that altars can be everywhere. I took the photo through an old Italian stone piece I had inserted into the stucco wall.

Page 79) Our minister, Charles Poole, gives us this benediction every communion Sunday. In the photograph of a European altar, the shadows make me feel the people have 'gone from this table' to 'all their other tables'.

REFERENCES

There are many floral artists featured in this book other than myself. Most of the altars are from my local church, Northminster Baptist. Other churches and artists are noted below by page numbers. The European cathedrals are in Italy, Germany, and Prague, Czech Republic.

Joe Rankin: p. 2, 12, 13, 14, 22, 23, 34, 35 (bottom right), 38, 39, 43, 47, 48, (right Side) 51, 52 (right) 53
Jane Gerber: p. 5, 58, 67, 73, 76 (right) (together with me)
Lida Carraway: p. 36
Jennifer Stribling: p. 42
Lisa Kelly: p. 1, 18, 19, 26, 30, 75
Ann Vickery: p. 1, 10, 11, 15, 19, 30, 59 (George Smith's sunflowers from Mississippi Delta hunting club)
Julia Sherwood: p. 70
John Tingle: p. 64
Linda Lambeth and Susan Brown: p 39
Irene Crowder: p. 74
Sally Yelverton: p. 76 (left)

Churches and Cathedrals
St James Episcopal: Jackson, Mississippi p. 4
First Baptist: Austin, Texas p. 21
Covenant Presbyterian: Jackson, Mississippi p. 33
Briarwood Presbyterian: Jackson, Mississippi p. 45 (vase and flowers in memory of Virginia Munford)
European Cathedral p. 3, 8, 49
European Altar p. 30, 60, 79
Cathedral in Prague p. 63
Chapel of the Cross: Madison, Mississippi p. 74
St Andrews Episcopal: Jackson, Mississippi p. 76
First Presbyterian, Nashville, Tennessee p. 77